BORN AGAIN NOW WHAT JESUS?

JOSEPH BRICE

Credits

Born Again Now What Jesus?
Published by BCMG
BCMG (Bridging the Conscience between Man and God), Inc.

Paperback
ISBN 979-8-224-71027-0

Library of Congress 2024
Unless otherwise indicated, Scripture quotations are from:

The HOLY BIBLE:

Table of Contents

Preface

Dear Reader,

I want to explain the incredible importance and power of being born again. This command is spoken for the first time in the Bible. Jesus describes the significance of this spiritual encounter to a religious leader who thought he was already saved and knew everything he needed to know about God.

This religious leader named Nicodemus, whom Jesus spoke to appeared shocked at the thought of this event being possible. Jesus clarifies that being born again is not a physical rebirth but a spiritual awakening that transforms one's life from the inside out.

The power of being born again restores us to God our Father and our original place before sin entered our hearts and contaminated our spirits. This spiritual rebirth determines who our eternal Father is, our family, and the kingdom we belong to.

Whether we like it or not, our existence is owed to our biological father. Whether we have a positive or negative relationship with them or have never met him, we are still his offspring. The seed we come from produces life; if appropriately tested, it can provide evidence of our paternity. This same principle also applies to our spiritual birth.

No one will enter the kingdom of God by mistake. Only those who have accepted Jesus Christ as their Savior and have been washed in His blood can enter His kingdom. If you have been born again, constantly feed your spirit by **praying, continuing in faith, studying, and meditating on God's word.**

The ultimate goal is to be converted and transformed by God's grace so we can help strengthen and support our fellow believers in their faith journey as part of our eternal family.

This profound experience can transform our lives and give us new direction, purpose, and meaning. It is a powerful reminder that we are more than just our physical bodies; we are spiritual beings with a divine purpose.

I hope this message resonates with you and inspires you to explore being born again even further.

Thank you for taking the time to read this.

May the love, joy, peace, and grace of our Lord Jesus cover you all.

Joseph Brice

Chapter One

Born Again

Born Again!

Being born again refers to a spiritual transformation and regeneration when someone accepts Jesus Christ as their Lord and Savior. When we experience spiritual rebirth, we inherit God's spiritual nature. We are a new creation in the spirit.

When a person becomes born again or is born of the spirit. Your flesh is not born again; your spirit and soul are. This fleshly body is destined to die once; after death is the judgment. The power of being born again is we get to judge ourselves when we are filled with God's Spirit; it doesn't matter what people think about us. It's what God, the devil, the angels, demons, hell, and the heavens know about you…you are born again! You are a child of the Most High God—a child of the king!

* * *

In the same way that a natural father impregnates a mother and gives birth to a newborn, we are the seed of our Heavenly Father, who is spirit. Regardless of any mistakes you may have made in the past, the miracle is that God no longer remembers them. In the spirit realm, you are given a brand new and clean slate to start afresh.

"Being born again" does not mean you will not make mistakes or do something wrong. It is quite the opposite. Just like a newborn baby, urination and bowel movements are not considered wrongdoings but are typical and expected. Similarly, in the spiritual realm, God does not get upset if we need a diaper change or cry because we are hungry or hurting. What mother or father would refuse their child of good things?

God doesn't expect us to love Him the way He loves us, at least not initially. When a baby is born, the parents are filled with excitement and joy to be in the presence of their newborn baby. Similarly, God is thrilled to have us in His presence. A newborn baby doesn't necessarily have to give anything to its parents except for its presence, which is a gift in itself. In the same way, our mere existence and presence are a precious gift to God when we are born again.

Heaven rejoices when even one soul comes to Jesus. God is not looking to find faults in a newborn soul but to love them. As a born-again Christian, you are a new creation, and old things have passed away. All things have become new.

As a newborn Christian, being vigilant about the person caring for you is crucial. Unfortunately, when abuse is all you've ever known, it can seem normal until someone comes along and shows you otherwise. Remember, we belong to God, and while we submit to authority, we will all answer to the highest authority in due time. God is the supreme of all.

Don't be overly concerned with those who may reject you. Understand that rejection is not personal, although it may be expressed through people you love or have been close to. You are born into a new kingdom where the king is Jesus. Studying His life will explain much of what you may have or possibly will suffer. Betrayal and hate are at the top of the list. This is not to frighten you but to prepare you for greatness.

* * *

You will not fit in with your old friends and crowds previously embraced. I know this may seem impossible, but God makes everything possible. When born again, you don't lose the memory of the mistakes you've made; you lose the penalty that came with those sins and are forgiven by God. This does not mean that you will not suffer some consequences of previous bad decisions or choices, but it does mean you are not in trouble with God. For example, you will be tested and tried like the apostle Paul, whose birth name was Saul. (read the books of Acts for reference).

Paul underwent a great deal of hardship due to his past actions of persecuting the church. However, his soul was ultimately saved, and he was elevated from being a self-righteous religious leader to becoming an apostle of Jesus Christ to the glory of God. Even though he was initially unaware of what an apostle was, he became one of the most significant figures in church history.

No matter what people tried to do to hurt or stop him, he always emerged victorious. The born-again experience is more than joining a church; it's about your newfound relationship with God, knowing you are a part of His divine plan. This story of Saul turned Paul is one of the most remarkable and authentic examples of the power of God's love, forgiveness, mercy, and grace, as Saul was the foremost adversary of the new church. No one persecuted the people of the Way (church) more than he did. Saul was the leading terrorist of the early church.

When Jesus met Saul on the road to Damascus, Saul was on his way to persecuting and killing members of the church. However, after appearing to Saul, Jesus spoke to him and explained that he was persecuting God and not just the people in the church. This encounter profoundly affected Saul, causing him to have a born-again experience. Before this event, Saul had been unaware of his prejudices and self-righteousness. As a Pharisee, he believed that he was the righteousness of God. However, this encounter with Jesus showed him how wrong he had been.

Saul was unaware that submitting to Jesus would allow him to be born again and see the kingdom of heaven and the true king, Jesus. Jesus was speaking to the hidden apostle within him. It takes the word of God to speak to one's true self.

We don't know who we are without the one who

created us. Saul, who became the apostle Paul, was a chosen vessel for God and didn't know it, and you could be, too. Saul was unaware that he had an apostle within him. Being born again and starting over gave him a new life and identity.

Do you know who is deep down within you? Do you know your true purpose for living? You could be living your life in church as Saul and not realize there is Paul within you, but you have to leave what you think is right and submit to the One who is righteous, Jesus. To know who you truly are, you must submit to God, be born again, and allow God to feed and nurture you to maturity; then, you will know what you were created to do. Being born again is more than saving ourselves; it's about growing in God to represent His kingdom and live a life dedicated to saving others. Somebody needs you and your God right now!

When you are born again, you receive a new spirit. And just like a newborn baby, you will get hungry and thirsty. It would be best if you were nourished with the fruits of the spirit. You must receive God's love and truthful teaching to be victorious rather than a victim.

* * *

We cannot experience being born again without God the Father. Jesus' death on the cross made what was previously impossible possible. The same person of Jesus who was present in the people (church) that Saul was trying to kill out of ignorance is the one who gave him a new life. Jesus' death was brutal, and He willingly submitted to that horrific death for you and me. This is the greatest expression of love ever shown! It is important to remember that the chance of being born again is only possible because of the ultimate sacrifice that Jesus made by dying for us.

After Jesus died, rather than breaking his legs like the others who were crucified, he was pierced in his side by the Roman soldiers. However, they had no clue they were fulfilling scripture, which was prophesied saying, *"The soldiers therefore came and broke the legs of the first man who had been crucified with Jesus, and then those of the other. But when they came to Jesus and found that he was already dead, they did not break his legs.*

Instead, one of the soldiers pierced Jesus' side with a spear, bringing a sudden flow of blood and water. The man who saw it has given testimony, and his testimony is true. He knows that he tells the truth and testifies so that you also may believe. These things happened so that the scripture would be fulfilled: "Not one of his bones will be broken," and, as another scripture says, "They will look on the one they have pierced." **John 19:32-37 NIV**

Out of Jesus came blood and water; this was the birthing of the church. The blood and water came from Jesus' heart. In other words, they pierced the heart of God by killing His Son. This was the beginning of our total and complete path to redemption. Jesus took on the sins of the world. Every sin committed and would be engaged in the future was in that blood. We are covered with His blood just as a natural baby when it is born of its mother.

If Jesus died for our sins and took on the punishment that comes with it, why would we continue to live in sin? When we receive Jesus, it is a spiritual rebirth that requires us to turn away from sinful behaviors and attitudes and fully dedicate our lives to following Jesus. In John 3:3, Jesus tells Nicodemus, "Truly, truly, I say to you, unless one is born again, he cannot see the kingdom of God." To be born again means to receive God's grace and forgiveness through faith in Christ. It is a supernatural work of the Holy Spirit that gives a person a new heart, mind, and spirit.

When you accept Jesus Christ as your Lord and Savior, you may experience people misunderstanding you, turning against you, or even hating you. This is because you now belong to a different kingdom - the kingdom of God. Previously, you belonged to the same kingdom as those people, but now you have a spiritual birthmark given to you by God that the devil recognizes. Regardless of age, gender, race, or economic status, if you encounter God and give your life to Christ, you may notice people treating you differently, sometimes as early as the next day. They may begin to distance themselves from you simply because you are now a different person spiritually.

This is why, as a born-again Christian, it may be hard to fit in with others who have not had this experience. It's like two different worlds colliding. Being born again means that you are no longer under Satan's dominion, and he has no legal right to you. Sin gives him power over your life. Therefore, if you live in sin, you are essentially putting Satan in the position of God in your life. The Holy Spirit is our comforter and our power!

When Jesus died on the cross to save us from our sins, death and the grave couldn't hold Him down. He emerged victorious from the grave and changed the game forever. As the Resurrection and the life, He conquered death and gave us the promise of eternal life. Those who believe in Jesus will never indeed die; we will be transformed into glory and gain a new home and family, with a body that will never fade or perish.

To be Born Again is to be in Him, and He is in us. Jesus is God and King, and He said, "Me and My Father are One and the Same." Just as we cannot separate the hydrogen and oxygen in water, we cannot separate Jesus from God. He is the ultimate example of love, grace, and power and offers salvation to all who believe in Him.

As we journey through life, we often become fixated on accumulating material possessions. But when we leave this world and cross over to eternity, we cannot take any of it. Our race, skin color, wealth, or poverty will not matter anymore. What will matter is what we carry within us -our spirit, soul, heart, and beliefs. Good or evil, they will define us in the "afterlife." Each of us is shaped by the spiritual force we choose to follow, be it the path of God or Satan's. Our choice determines the course of our life and the person we become.

Our works will also accompany us; although they do not save us, we will be judged for them. Ultimately, it is not about what we own but what we become. That is why being Born Again is so crucial. It is the only way to receive the Holy Spirit and become like God, having His nature and characteristics. We become sons and daughters of The Most High God. So, do not be overly concerned about those who may not understand you. Instead, focus on your Heavenly Father who created you. If there is anyone who understands you, it is Him.

Our true family is made up of those who have been reborn in faith, not those who attend church for the sake of it. This is why the movement in the Book of Acts was so remarkable. Despite facing persecution and hatred, the believers held love for one another. They knew the world despised them for the same reasons, and they hated the true prophets and Jesus.

* * *

This world is where we are tested and where we choose which kingdom we belong to and who our God and Father will be.

Jesus was sent to expose the devil who has been hiding on this earth and committing all kinds of corruptible deeds. We were unaware of his actions for a long time. However, now that he can no longer hide, he is angry. If you are Born Again, you must stop trying to fit in with the world because you will never belong there. Instead, as Born-Again Christians, you are no longer slaves to sin but kings and priests of the kingdom of God.

It can be frustrating when people you love seem uneasy around you or when you're suddenly excluded from social events you used to attend. But as followers of God, we need to support and accept each other through thick and thin. Keep your faith and walk with Jesus, knowing that "He will never leave nor forsake you."

Trust that these people will come around eventually if they belong to God. Remember, no one who belongs to God will be left behind.

This is a fact: if anyone in this world belongs to God, no matter what path they may be on or what evil they may be entangled in, they will eventually obey God's voice and be converted. You're born again; now what? Be a living example of Christ and be encouraged in your new walk and life with Him. Know that you are part of a different kingdom that will last forever.

As believers, we have allowed the enemy in disguise to reduce our faith to a mere religion, forgetting that Jesus came to expose and destroy the works of the devil. Jesus did not come to this world to start a new religion; this is a great deception from the enemy. He came to restore us to our original place as sons and daughters of the Most High God.

Remember, Satan was called "the prince of this world," but Jesus is the King of everything. Let us not forget that we are kings and priests, empowered to live a life of purpose and fulfillment. So, let us focus on the true meaning of Jesus' message and strive to live our lives according to His teachings. Jesus said, "I came that you may have life and live it fully."

Becoming born again is a spiritual process that

involves turning away from sin and dedicating your life to following Jesus Christ;

- **Repent of your sins— This means acknowledging your sinful nature and avoiding harmful behaviors and attitudes. Make a decision to change and make Jesus the Lord of your life.**

- **Believe in Jesus Christ— Accept that Jesus died on the cross to pay for your sins and rose again from the dead. Have faith that you can be forgiven and have eternal life through his sacrifice.**

- **Confess your faith— Openly declare your belief in Jesus by saying, "I confess with my mouth that Jesus is Lord and believe in my heart that God raised him from the dead."**

- **Be baptized— Being baptized by immersion symbolizes your death from sin and new life in Christ. It is an outward expression of your inner commitment.**

- **Read and study the Bible—The Bible guides**

our lives as Christians. Set aside time to read it daily and apply its teachings.

- **Worship and fellowship—Attend church services to worship God and connect with other believers. Fellowship helps you grow spiritually, and you should never forget to serve others.**

- **Pray—Talk to God regularly to develop a consistent prayer life. Pray for guidance and strength, and share the gospel.**

- **Witness to others— Tell others about your faith in Jesus, what he has done in your faith in Jesus, and what he has done in your life. Share the good news of salvation.**

- **New life in Christ—Experiencing spiritual rebirth and a new relationship with God**

- **Seeking to follow Jesus— Living for Christ and His purposes rather than self.**

- **Eternal life— Knowing you have the gift of salvation and will spend eternity with God**

The Born Again experience brings a new spiritual birth and transformed life. It is a lifelong journey of growth in Jesus Christ. Are you ready to tap into the power of the Holy Spirit and become a born-again believer?

Discover the revelations of Jesus Christ and who we are in Him with **"Born Again, Now What?"** This book will empower you to take control of your life to become a ruler of righteousness, not a follower of anything contrary to the will of God.

Chapter Two

My Heart Belongs

In summary, being born again involves a dramatic change of heart and mind that results in a personal relationship with Jesus Christ. It marks the beginning of a new life lived for God's glory.

Why come to God to be born again if you don't change how you live? You cannot be raised in the spirit by transgressors of God's word and will and think it's ok because it's not. You must be intentional about who teaches you and inspire your life. You must have a prayer life, read God's word, know that your Bible is your new best friend, and stay in communication with Jesus. Know who he is to you and who you are to him. You are now betrothed to Jesus Christ and are his life and future. You do not belong to Satan anymore and should not have been his in the first place, but because of sin, we were in bondage to sin and its nature.

* * *

Why get married if you continue to live a single life? It is unfair to the one in the marriage who truly loves you and wants to be married. Jesus is the one in this relationship that loves you and wants to be married. He's not looking for a fling-thing, hook-up, or side-chick. If you are a Christian and continue to live a life of sin and spiritual promiscuity, regardless of positions and titles, you are abusing mercy, grace, and Jesus.

All of these were present when you were born again and knew the love invested in your new life. Likewise, in an earthly marriage, we have witnesses when we make our vows to each other. Spiritual adultery in our relationship with God is so easy because it is a common practice in our natural marriages. One day, we all will stand before God and give an account for our adulterous relationships if we don't repent.

Don't be deceived; God is not to be mocked; whatsoever we sow, that is what we will reap." Whether pastors, bishops, praise and worship leaders, or laypeople, we are sheep; Jesus is our shepherd, and our life is not ours. If you continue to do the things you used to do before being born again, then it means you are spiritually separated from God. Anointing is like having a wedding ring stating that you are married and then taking it off when you want to be perceived as single.

Many claim to be spiritual representatives of Christ, but their actions tell a different story. They behave as if they are single when they are not around other devout Christians or attending church. However, in the company of fellow believers, they put on a show of being in love with Jesus as if it were an act. This kind of behavior is not genuine and goes against what Jesus taught. He made it clear that those who love Him will follow His teachings.

If we are indeed married to Christ, why are we so desperate to be accepted by the world? It's time for us to remain faithful to Him and not seek approval from a society that doesn't know Him. Unfortunately, many who are anointed keep company with others who are anointed cheaters on Jesus and love his blessings more than they love Him.

The anointing is like your engagement ring, the sign and evidence of your engagement saying you are spoken for. It is worn to show who we are betrothed to, but we justify cheating because we have not yet gone to heaven for the wedding. Maybe we do it out of selfishness or ignorance; we are cheaters… spiritual cheaters, and the angels are recording our actions to show the evidence of infidelity to Jesus, who is the groom. This is the sign of why we have so many divorces, "there's nothing new under the sun." What's taking place in the natural that we can see is the indicator of what is taking place in the spiritual that we can't see.

In my Father's house are many mansions: if it were not so, I would have told you. I am going to prepare a place for you. And if I go and prepare a place for you, I will come again, and receive you unto myself; that where I am, there ye may be also. **John 14:2-3 KJV**

In the meanwhile, Jesus is working on our behalf for a great life and future, and the jealous ex, who is the devil, is on a rampage trying to give a reason for the wedding to be called off. Don't think for a moment that Satan will not hesitate to testify against any of us if he gets us to violate our relationship with Jesus Christ.

* * *

Jesus is faithful in this relationship and expects us to be faithful. You know Satan can't have you for one minute and not tell. The devil wants you and me to be excommunicated from God and heaven. He wants to steal your crown; don't let him have what belongs to you.

No matter who you are and how long you may have belonged to a church or maybe pastoring like Nicodemus, a priest who received the gift of God through Jesus Christ and started over by accepting the miracle of being Born Again. Only this time, with deep sincerity, be dedicated to the One True God. Take on His nature and love, and be faithful, trustworthy, dedicated, and devoted to Him. Why not make up your mind today who you will serve and rededicate your life to the one who truly loves you, and that is, without doubt, Jesus?

"He came unto his own, and his own didn't receive him. But as many as received him, to them gave he the power to become the sons and daughters of God, even to them that believe on his name: which were born, not of "blood, nor of the will of the flesh, nor the will of man, but of God." John 1: 11-13

Chapter Three

Choose Jesus

Jesus died so that we could have eternal power and authority over all of the enemy through the Spirit of God within us. It's time to stop waiting for Jesus to return and live a life of purpose and power. Let's unite and turn this world right side up. Jesus is not just a religion but God and King of kings. If you are born again, now is the time to step into your destiny and become who you were meant to be. Don't wait any longer; the power is within you!

Have you ever wondered who Jesus was? Who was he if he wasn't the Son of God, the Messiah, the Resurrection? And why would the "powers that be" of the entire world agree to start time over? It's a question worth exploring. What need was there to mess with time, to change time? These are important questions that deserve thoughtful consideration. Let's delve deeper into this mystery and uncover the truth.

* * *

Here's a valuable insight I'd like to share with you from my experience: The devil only tempts you with things that you have not yet overcome. For instance, if drugs are your weakness, he will try to use anyone to bring drugs your way. Similarly, if relationships are your weakness, he will try to make someone contact you, even if it's not for any good reason. Although such people may appear gentle and caring, the truth is that Satan wants you back.

Not because he loves you but because he hates you and wants to destroy you. However, once you have truly overcome the devil, the sins, and the relationships of the past, he will not bring those things to you anymore. He will have to look for new things that may tempt you. Satan is constantly searching the desires of your heart. He throws things at you to see what sticks or gets the most significant reaction.

It's essential to learn how to manage your life proactively instead of just reacting to challenges. The enemy is always looking for ways to undermine your faith and calling, so it's essential to be vigilant and not give him any ammunition. When you have honestly let go of any relationships that may end your spiritual journey, the enemy won't be able to use them against you, as he knows they no longer have power over you. It's crucial to stay strong and rooted in your faith.

Temptation can be made of things you may have desired in the past, but now that you have found Christ, these things no longer fit in your life. It's essential to learn to move on and keep your enemies in their place - where God intended them to be. You must stop making it so easy for the devil to destroy you. If the relationship didn't work when you both were on the devil's side, how can it work now when only one of you is submitted to Jesus? If your partner is not in love with Jesus, they will not be in love with you loving Jesus. The devil's job is to get you away from Jesus, just like he got Judas away.

You cannot serve two masters. So choose today who you will serve and be faithful!

Chapter Four

Born Again Now What?

Being born again leads to a changed life. The believer experiences a new nature, desire for righteousness, and growth in the likeness of Christ. Being born again involves humility and repentance, which involves surrendering one's life to Christ. Like a new born it takes time to grow. You won't get it all in one day. Don't mistake mistakes for being wicked. Any new born is weak, it takes time to get strong and God understands this, don't be discouraged when you are new to this and make a mistake, the devil will be present to speak through some to say, I thought you were saved or a Christian? This is the devil's mockery.

It is important to strengthen your relationship with

your Heavenly Father. You can achieve this by praying, fasting, reading, and meditating on His word day and night, no matter what. When we are Born Again, we become children of God. He then spends time with us through His word and presence, seeking Him. He abides with us and prepares a place for us. As we grow, having Him with us should become our norm.

Communicating with God in the face of the many temptations surrounding us is essential. If you observe people who are passionate about their faith, you will notice that individuals often try to undermine that passion, even within the church. The church is not the kingdom itself but rather a community of people who belong to the kingdom. However, counterfeit versions and a black market will always exist, just like anything that holds value. The church is no exception.

It is important to take to heart the warnings that Jesus taught and gave to His disciples on many occasions. Failure to understand how much the devil wants to bring you back into his kingdom and work for him may lead him to use anyone or vessel to achieve your frustration with the church, people, and eventually God if you are not adequately equipped.

Many people do not understand this and leave the church in significant percentages. While some make it back, others, like Judas, do not.

Listen to what Jesus tells His disciples and how this applies to us as His followers and in this generation, *"When an unclean spirit comes out of a person, it goes through arid places seeking rest and does not find it. Then it says, 'I will return to the house I left.' When it arrives, it finds the house unoccupied, swept clean, and put in order. Then it takes seven other spirits more wicked than itself, and they go in and live there. And the final condition of that person is worse than the first. "That is how it will be with this wicked generation."* **Matthew 12:43-45 NIV**

There are people on earth who may hold beliefs contrary to God. However, it is important to remember that they were not always this way. Some may even say, "I used to go to church, but now I'm done with that. They made me believe everything was a sin. I want to do what I want to do." What happens is that when people stop praying and believing due to disappointments, their spiritual life becomes empty. God cleanses our hearts and souls, casting out unclean spirits when we get saved. Our hearts become a house filled with the things of God.

The unclean spirit that previously lived in you is now homeless and may have been with you since childhood; this spirit has occupied your soul. These are principalities…former princes from the kingdom of God who were cast down. *"Put on the whole armor of God, that ye may be able to stand against the wiles of the devil. For we wrestle not against flesh and blood, but against principalities, against powers, against the rulers of the darkness of this world, against spiritual wickedness in high places."* **Ephesians 6:11-12**

These spirits know the principles of the kingdom and how they work, whether good or evil, if adequately utilized. Their job is to disqualify an individual, sowing seeds of doubt and ultimately turning to unbelief. Doubt is not a sin, but unbelief is; anyone can doubt, and that's a seed, but unbelief is the result of doubt, which is uninterrupted and becomes unified with evil and reckless thoughts turned into actions. The fruit of the seed of doubt has become the fruit of unbelief. Seed is sown into the mind, but unbelief comes from meditation on it until it matures and produces evil fruit, which can only happen if it is in the heart. You must believe the lie for the devil to work it and use you against the things of God and His will.

Now that God's belongings are no longer in your house, which He cleaned (the heart), the unclean spirit checks on you like an ex because he could not find anyone like you. You would listen to, entertain, and make him feel comfortable with his uncleanness; he misses home. He returns to check on his old address, which is your heart, and finds it available.

He is so excited at the thought of moving back in that before someone gets the individual to seek God again, he gets reinforcement, seven other spirits dirtier and more wicked than he is. He cannot afford to lose his house again; they have entered and taken over. This kind of person will find it hard to pray, read the Bible, go to church, and focus on the things of God that used to bring them joy that came so naturally. They will not only have no desire to pray and read God's word but will get irritated at the thought of seeking God all over again.

This is what makes it so very hard for the

backslidden Christian. I used to be you, and I was sick and tired of that devil and those demons. I found myself doing things I would have never imagined. It took me years to figure this out, but I did it with God's grace, mercy, and help. One day, I cried out to the Lord for help because I knew this wasn't me; I wouldn't do these things. People mock people when they say, "The devil made me do it!" not all are lying.

When you struggle to find time to pray and read God's word, it could be a sign that you are at risk of losing touch with your spiritual self. Prayer is a means of communicating with God, and the enemy seeks to sever this connection between you and your spiritual family. It's worth considering that things might have turned out differently if Judas had been praying instead of chasing after money. Instead, he led the enemy to Jesus while he was in the anointed place of prayer, the Garden of Gethsemane, where he earnestly sought God's guidance.

If Judas had not stopped praying, he would not have allowed doubt to turn into disbelief. Why? Judas wanted a king, prosperity, and notoriety, but Jesus took him too long. Whatever your plight, the devil is constantly knocking at your door to see if your place is available again. Judas was saved (first stage) but didn't stay long enough to mature and be converted; there's a difference. Peter denied Jesus but remained for the next stage, which was being converted. Therefore, He became the apostle Peter rather than" the son of perdition." Don't allow the enemy to rob you of your next with God. Stay with God; in a thousand years from now, you'll be glad you did. Imagine where Peter is right now compared to Judas.

As Christians and believers, we have the Holy Spirit within us and, therefore, should not struggle with doubts about eternal life, the existence of angels or demons, or supernatural encounters with God. When we were born, we inherited a rebellious and contrary nature towards God due to Adam's sin of disobedience. This sin has separated us from God, our Father, and threatens our eternal life. It causes harm and robs us of peace, joy, and wholeness. Being Born Again gives us a new start and restoration of all things lost, especially our relationship with God.

The family of God and His kingdom is not something you can join; you have to be born into it. To understand the realm of royalty, you have to have royal blood. Kings are not elected; they are born. Born a king, raised as a prince with the understanding that the ultimate is becoming the king of rule. We are God's Royal Priesthood, kings and priests only ordained by God.

The power of being Born Again is that Jesus' blood becomes ours. When He died on the cross, our blood became His, and His blood dominated. By enslaving our place, He allowed us to take His place as a king. Jesus knew exactly what He was doing, and His resurrection made Him the first of His kind. When we see Him, we will become beings of light and perfection, just like Him. So, don't let anything discourage you from your belief in Christ. Whatever you may be going through, your best days are ahead. Being Born Again gives the believer the power to become children of God by blood. Let the redeemed of the Lord say, "So!"

When we are born again, it's a spiritual birth, and we inherit the spiritual nature of God. It is the primary reason for you not fitting in with others, especially those who have not encountered being born again. This is the clash of two different natures, characteristics, and kingdoms. As Being Born-Again, you have been snatched from the devil, his darkness and kingdom, because he no longer has a legal right to you. Sin gives the devil legal rights to your life. Operating in a sinful nature without resistance grants him the authority to be your god.

Receiving the Holy Spirit is our Comforter in our infancy stage and continues with us as we grow in grace. Still, as we mature in God, we should experience its power and ability to lead, guide, and connect us to God, angels, and eternity without restrictions marked by time. Christ should be at the helm of our existence.

During his ministry, Jesus spoke about the availability of the kingdom to those who believe. He explained that there are three stages to gaining access to the kingdom. The first stage is that it is "at hand," which means it is available to you. The second stage is "upon you," meaning you have gained access and are experiencing the benefits of the kingdom, such as healings, deliverances, and miracles. The third stage is that the kingdom is "now within you," which means that you are a part of it and that the supernatural part of God is in you.

However, despite this, many Christians struggle to

believe other believers when they claim to have had visitations from angels or Jesus. This is perplexing because, as believers, we are part of the kingdom, and Christ and the angels are in it. Why wouldn't angels, or any other beings from the kingdom who serve God, be available to believers? Angels are appointed to us for protection and service, but it's important to remember not to worship them. We should honor and respect them as servants and messengers of God and recognize who they are in the kingdom, but our worship should be directed only to God.

Jesus said, You will see greater things than this, I assure you and most solemnly say to you, you will see heaven opened and the angels of God ascending and descending on the Son of Man [the bridge between heaven and earth]. **John 1: 50-51 AMP**

In the Bible, the first time Jesus spoke about being "Born Again" was to a Pharisee, a leader in Israel who was respected and known as a teacher in Jerusalem among the chief priests. His name was Nicodemus. It's interesting because this priest was considered a holy man who taught people about God. But Jesus told him that he needed to be born again. The priest didn't understand what Jesus meant and asked if he was supposed to go back into his mother's womb.

Jesus explained that being born again meant being spiritually reborn, not physically. He was telling the priest that, even though he was a spiritual leader, he was too focused on physical things. Jesus reminded him that as a leader of Israel, he should know the importance of being spiritually minded and being born again.

Some bishops, pastors, and leaders have been saved for many years but have become infected with an arrogant spirit of religion. As a result, they do not feel the need to repent and be born again, even though it is precisely what they need to do. They may know how to do church and maintain religious practices, but they cannot see the kingdom of God, just as Nicodemus could not. Despite all the things Jesus did in his ministry, he never cast out a spirit of religion.

The religious person must denounce the spirit of judgment by humbling themselves to God and asking for forgiveness for attempting to usurp God's authority over His people. It requires surrendering oneself to God to invite Him into their hearts. God does not coexist with the devil. Many preachers operate from their anointing rather than God's glory. Satan deceives them into believing that God has not rejected them due to their anointing. However, this means that they will not enter heaven upon their death.

It is important to constantly examine our hearts for pride, regardless of how long we have been a part of a church community. We should repent and ask for God's transformation to make us new. We can pray and say, "Lord, please forgive me for my sins and allow me to be born again." This prayer can open our eyes to the truth and reveal God's true nature. Remember, the church is the people and not the building. We should focus on serving others to serve God rather than just attending services. The ultimate goal is to be a part of God's kingdom.

If you genuinely love God, humbling yourself before Him will be honorable. However, if you have the spirit of Lucifer inside you, it will enrage you. Have you ever wondered about the fate of the religious leaders who lied about Jesus and manipulated the law to have Him condemned and crucified? Are they at peace, sitting at the table with Jesus in heaven, or in a holding cell in Hell waiting for their court date to be taken before The White Throne Judgment? What do you think… I would like to know your opinion on this matter.

It's not on record that he openly told a thief, a murderer, a liar, a drunk, a prostitute, or any other sinner that they needed to be born again because they did not wrestle with theology or religious studies as the priests would. These people were hungry and thirsty for God and needed his help; they were ready to receive God without contest. When sinners accept God and receive His Spirit, this is a spiritual new birth. They are born again, even if they don't understand what has happened to them or know what it's called.

What Jesus left on record for us is that the most complex people to humble themselves and receive God holistically are those who have studied God and hold high positions of spiritual authority in churches and other facilities where they can be used to teach people about a God they have not experienced or encountered. This kind of leader will teach that the Holy Spirit was a thing of the past, and encounters we read about in the Bible happened back then, but God does not operate like this in the present day.

* * *

Like Nicodemus, they have not had a rebirth from God, and neither are they a part of God. These false teachers may as well teach that God is dead if He cannot do in this generation what He did in past generations; know this about God: He is God of all generations, and "there is nothing too hard for God!" Why go to church in the first place if God has lost His power and is the God of the dead?

Do you remember what Jesus said, *"About the resurrection of the dead—have you not read what God said to you, 'I am the God of Abraham, the God of Isaac, and the God of Jacob'? He is not the God of the dead but of the living."* God didn't say, "He was the God of, or used to be." "God is the same yesterday, today, and forevermore." He is the same God!

Many pastors and leaders have never been born again, although they regularly teach and preach to congregations. Jesus said, "You must be born again" to the so-called "holy man." This would be equivalent to Jesus talking to a Bishop, Pastor, or Pope in our day and time. In essence, Jesus was telling him he needed to start over. Many pastors and church leaders have studied God, learned about God, and carried God's word (the Bible), but they do not know God.

Nicodemus was confused about who Jesus was, even though he saw manifestations of the Holy Spirit, which he studied in the Tora and Prophets, as signs of the coming of the Messiah, about his characteristics and powers. Even being a witness to all of his works, the priest continued to struggle with theology over facts.

For example, some people are passionate fans of celebrities from all genres. They may have pictures, posters, movies, music, clothing, and other items related to their favorite stars. They can also tell you almost everything about their idols. However, the truth is that if you were to ask them if they have ever met their favorite celebrity, they would disappointingly tell you that they have never met them in person. Fans' information about their favorite celebrities is merely based on collected data and research.

Similarly, many pastors and leaders who preach the gospel have never had any interaction or encounters with Jesus or His Holy Spirit. They pass on information to others they may have been taught or believe to be accurate without firsthand experience or knowledge. Their persuasiveness can be so compelling that one may be misled into thinking they are close to God and have a personal relationship with Jesus. Let us strive to seek the truth and knowledge on our own to establish a genuine connection with our Lord Jesus Christ.

We understand that attending church or congregations is important. However, it is equally important to understand the spirit of the person teaching you about Jesus and how well they can help you work through His teachings. God intends to use you for His glory and not just to have you read or talk about the people of the Bible. If you possess His Spirit, you can do what His Spirit empowers you to do. You should not limit yourself. Being born again is a powerful experience because you are born into His kingdom and receive His Holy Spirit and Christ's blood in your spirit. Being a faithful follower of Jesus is more than just being a mere fan.

Jesus also taught him the difference between the kingdom and religion, attending services versus being a servant of God, one who is willing to serve the people rather than esteeming himself above people looking to be served. Jesus lets him know why it was so hard for him to understand and see God when it is right there in his face. You can join a church, temple, or even a ministry, but you must be born again to be in the kingdom of God; the kingdom is not something or a place you can join or become a member of.

Although Nicodemus saw scriptures being fulfilled that had been prophesied many years prior, such as where the Messiah would be born, a little town called Bethlehem, being a Nazarite to the Lord, being born of a virgin, the son of David, being rejected by his people, healing the sick, opening the eyes of the blind, being a shepherd of love and compassion to a loss and left people, one who would answer all their questions and solving eternal mysteries concerning God. He would bring God to the people without reservations. Jesus did all these things at this point, and the leaders continued not to believe.

The coming of the Messiah was the very foundation of the people, and even if the religious leaders did not witness it with their own eyes, they heard about the things happening. They had enough witnesses to know whether Jesus was an impostor or not. These religious leaders are struggling to accept

Jesus as the Messiah because he doesn't fit into their imagination. It is important not to miss what God has for you because it doesn't appear or look like what you have been waiting and believing for.

Could this be the answer to our prayers? Jesus was their answer, but they were looking for something else. They waited on another Messiah, another fulfillment that fit the narrative and their imagination of what God should look like, what the Son of God should look like, what the Messiah should look like, or what about the coming of the Son of Man or the Son of God would have we imagined?

Jesus did not come into this world to start a new religion or save the devil and his followers. He came to expose the devil's works so he couldn't hide anymore. He gave his life and died to save humanity, to save us who all believe in him and put our trust in him, and then he will take us home to his kingdom, which is our kingdom. You may wonder how people can lie, know the truth, and even go to court, put their hand on the Bible, and swear in the name of God that they are telling the truth, the whole truth. Nothing but the truth and then lie; what makes a good liar?

* * *

It is said that a great liar knows the truth, the whole truth, and uses it to their advantage. However, we must understand that the devil also uses people to spread lies. In such situations, Jesus advises us not to be anxious about what we say, for our Heavenly Father will guide us. We should not be surprised when we encounter people who lie effortlessly, especially in court or when it concerns money or other worldly things. Those who do the devil's work are his children and speak his language. Jesus wants us to understand this and not be shocked by the works of the devil, but instead, we should strive to destroy his works and be separated from him.

When you become a born-again Christian, you may experience people turning against you and hating you. This is because you now belong to a different kingdom, the kingdom of God. You have a spiritual birthmark given to you by God, and the devil knows this mark.

Whether you are a child, an adolescent, a young adult, an adult, or a senior, your age doesn't matter. You may go to work the next day after encountering God on Sunday and giving your life to Christ, and people will start treating you differently without even mentioning that you gave your life to Christ. They may start withdrawing themselves from you because you are now a different creature spiritually.

Being a unique creation can feel like you are an alien to others. They may not be able to comprehend you and may feel uneasy in your presence. You may be excluded from social groups that you were once a part of and may wonder why you are no longer invited to events, despite having done nothing wrong.

This is why the people of God need to embrace one another. Your true family consists of those who have been born again, not those who are merely faking it or attending church out of habit. This is why the movement in the Book of Acts was so remarkable. Despite being persecuted and hated, the believers loved one another. They understood that the world hated them because it first hated the true prophets and Jesus. This world is our proving ground, where we determine what kingdom, we belong to and who will be our God and Father.

Jesus was sent to expose the devil who has been hiding on this earth and committing all kinds of corruptible deeds. We were unaware of his actions for a long time. However, now that he can no longer hide, he is angry. If you are Born Again, you must stop trying to fit in with the world because you will never belong there. Instead, as a born-again Christian, you belong to God and his kingdom. It's important to understand that the devil has his kingdom and followers who will spend eternity with him. These individuals engage in evil deeds, and they destroy communities, people, families, and even churches. As a result, they are different from us, and we must not entangle ourselves with them, trying to be accepted.

They are of another creation. They are the children of darkness and will never do what's right, no matter the consequences. They are obsessed with buying good things, although they are evil. They don't have a good heart or good intentions; they are selfish and wicked, and they are doing the will of their father, which is the devil.

No matter what you do, they will never love or accept you. If they do not accept Jesus as they have, the fight is on; their assignment given to them by Satan is to get them to denounce God as Judas did. You will have to denounce God, divorce him to get things from the devil on a whole other level, and get on his payroll; he wants to be your source, and this is why weak people sell their souls.

If we're not careful, we might worship a dressed-up and made-up lost soul hiding behind material things purchased with money. Some people are dying while they are living and selling their souls for a compliment. This is all they live for to be praised and worshipped. Wanting too many people to like them that's too much power to give to any potential enemy.

This is the Devil's greatest weakness. He desires your praise and worship; he desperately wants to be God. Being born again and taught God's word without false doctrine will open your eyes to the kingdom's truth. Don't be afraid of what you see. It's not the devil, and you are not crazy.

We think we know people, maybe not as well as we believe; *Jesus said, "Do not think that I have come to bring peace to the earth. I have not come to bring peace but a sword, for I have come to set a man against his father, and a daughter against her mother, and a daughter-in-law against her mother-in-law. And a person's enemies will be those of his own household.*

* * *

Whoever loves father or mother more than me is not worthy of me, and whoever loves son or daughter more than me is not worthy of me. And whoever does not take his cross and follow me is not worthy of me. Whoever finds his life will lose it, and whoever loses his life for my sake will find it." Mathew 10: 34-39

This applies to every one of us: If you have not been born again, then according to Jesus, you are considered an enemy of God. On the day of judgment, Satan will present evidence against you, and you will be judged accordingly. Therefore, it is essential to understand the significance of being born again and its importance.

When you are born again, and others are not, it is possible for loved ones who belong to the other kingdom may hate you without understanding why. It does not matter whether they attend church; to be considered true family, they must belong to the same kingdom as you. I am a living testimony to this truth; those who do not belong to God's kingdom can turn on you. Human effort cannot fix this situation; it is beyond our control. Only God has the power to remedy it.

* * *

Jesus is the truth himself; that's why he always spoke truthfully. It's unsurprising if people you thought loved you hate you. They might have been pretending, and their father could be the devil if they hadn't accepted God in their lives. This is not just a ceremony; it's about loving each other and being a part of God's eternal family. Love never fails, so try to see things through the eyes of the Holy Spirit and use discernment to understand what's happening.

You'll notice that God is absent in the eyes of those against you. This doesn't mean that we should become judgmental, but we should be aware of what's happening around us so that we don't give in to the pressures they put on us. Jesus has exposed the enemy so the devil cannot hide from the Holy Spirit. There are two kingdoms; if you look carefully, you'll see who belongs to which.

I witnessed people who used to preach, pray, fast, and lay their hands on people turned away from God because He took too long to bless them the way they wanted to be blessed. They became offended and disappointed because God did not show up for them in a materialistic way. He did not give them the pleasures of the flesh like they imagined the blessings should have brought them.

They wanted to use God rather than allowing God to use them, and for this reason, they turn on God and His people; they will hate you for loving the Lord and preaching the gospel; they will hate you for choosing God over them, they are deceived into thinking this is a competition as if they can compete with God. They will hate you for even talking about God or mentioning His name, and that's why we must be careful that we do not allow the world to turn our relationship with our Heavenly Father into a religion. Where you can't talk about religion, you can talk about your Father. If you're Born Again, Now What? Where do I go from here? What do I do with my days as a new Born-Again Believer? What do I do with my time because everything is different?

Being Born Again is powerful because while we cannot choose our natural parents, we get to choose our Heavenly Father and accept Christ as our Savior. Looking around humanity, we see every human being was born through a woman. It is a universal truth that every human, regardless of race, creed, religion, politics, education, or occupation, entered this world through a woman. However, when we go to heaven, we will all have one thing in common - we came through God through His spirit. This is what unites us in the Kingdom of God. If you're not, you are an alien and don't belong there.

Everybody is not going to heaven because they do not belong there. Evil does not belong in heaven, nor can sin exist there. This is why Lucifer and the other angels were kicked out; they were kicked out before their sins had a chance to manifest; the evil hidden in them is being exposed every day in this world by way of every race and generation. Some are worse than others, but manifestations for sure. It would be in comparison to trying to live in a place where there is no air. If you carry or supply your air, eventually, the air will run out. Evil cannot survive in heaven because it has nothing to feed it, nothing to nurture it. There was nothing in heaven to promote evil, darkness, sins, or transgressions.

Now that you're born again, pray consistently, read God's word, study God's word, meditate on His word both day and night, gain strength, and grow in grace. Mature in God to the point that the devil knows he will get hell messing with you, as he did with Jesus,

* * *

He shouted at the top of his voice, "What do you want with me, Jesus, Son of the Most High God? In God's name, don't torture me!" For Jesus had said to him, "Come out of this man, you impure spirit!" Then Jesus asked him, "What is your name?" "My name is Legion," he replied, "for we are many." And he begged Jesus again and again not to send them out of the area. **Mark 5:7-10 NIV**

Your Holy Ghost is like a fiery furnace, a fury not to be played with.

Read God's word until you see yourself in the word, be confident, be stable, and unmovable in God's love no matter what the enemy tries to do to you. His works against you are temporary; you will have the victory and the last word. Your enemies will be cut down like grass, so pray for them and leave it in God's hands. Love God with all of your heart; let no one or anything change that hate them back. You may have to keep your distance. People will leave you because you will not leave God, and that's how powerful being born again is.

* * *

People will leave you; spouses may divorce you or cheat on you with someone less than you or maybe someone who used to be close to you because the devil is working through them, trying to get a carnal, worldly, and ungodly reaction from you. In hopes of you going back to your old life, which is the Old Serpent called the Devil and Hell. Do not react but pro-act. Don't be predictable.
It would be best if you weren't shocked at their behavior because you said I did a good thing.

Yes, you did. I gave my life to Christ. Yes, you did, and welcome to the family of God. Being Born Again is the greatest thing you can do in your life because you establish who your Father is, where your home is, and who your family is. When you're Born Again, you belong to the family of God, and I would like to say welcome to the family of God. You are Born Again; Now What?

"Put on the whole armor of God so that you can stand against the devil's schemes. Our struggle is not against flesh and blood but against the rulers, against the authorities, against the powers of this dark world, and against the spiritual forces of evil in the heavenly realms.

* * *

Therefore, put on the whole armor of God so that when the day of evil comes, you may be able to stand your ground and, after you have done everything, stand.

Stand firm then, with the belt of truth buckled around your waist, the breastplate of righteousness in place, and your feet fitted with the readiness that comes from the gospel of peace. In addition to all this, take up the shield of faith, with which you can extinguish all the flaming arrows of the evil one.

Take the helmet of salvation and the sword of the Spirit, which is the word of God. And pray in the Spirit on all occasions with all kinds of prayers and requests. With this in mind, be alert and always pray for all the saints." *Ephesians 6:11-18*

Born Again Now What Jesus? Answer: No matter what comes our way, we should understand that God is preparing, training, and making us warriors for His kingdom. We are to fight to deliver those who are in some of the same bondages that we used to be entangled in before experiencing God's grace and mercy…before we were born again.

We are to pray for our enemies; I know this can be

a hard one to do and may even seem ridiculous because of how evil people can be but pray for them anyway. This is what Jesus asks us, who are born again, to do. It's for Him, not necessarily for us or them; we pray for them for Him. This will leave a mark of God on them if they do not take heed to the warnings.

God will reward you for doing this for Him. We may never know if the one who hates us the most could possibly hear the word of God and be converted like Saul, who became the apostle Paul. Your enemy today could possibly be one of the greatest missionaries for Christ in this generation if they get some prayer and love.

Jesus said, "Love your enemies and bless them who curse you." These two commands have to be the most challenging for us who are Born-Again Believers.

"Born Again Now What Jesus?"

Imagine Jesus answering this question: *"I want you to spiritually mature and grow up so you can have authority to; Live like Me, Love like Me, and Lead like Me."*

* * *

"But to as many as received and welcomed Him, He gave the right [the authority, the privilege] to become children of God, that is, to those who believe in (adhere to, trust in, and rely on) His name." *John 1:12 AMP*

Born to be an extension of Jesus on earth until He comes...

Chapter Five

It's a Relationship

Live for God, be like God, love like God, be excited, and look forward to loving people while spreading the good news of the kingdom until it's your time to leave this world. When you leave this world, you will be reunited and united with your actual family, the family of God, those who have been praying for you and cheering you on because they preceded you in this world and fought so they understand how challenging it can be. To the Born Again Believer, remember this: death is not your enemy or punishment; death is your servant, your transportation, your Uber to heaven, rejoice you are going home.

In all fairness, we cannot expect people, on average, to understand us when we become born again when we see on record how a priest didn't. We have much more information and testimonials on the subject, but most importantly, we must understand it's spiritual. Being misunderstood is common, but it doesn't become evil until people attempt to destroy you or your faith in God. People becoming aggressive and destructive is a sign of negative influence. Seek support from like-minded individuals. Surround yourself with other Born Again Believers.

This is vitally important for the new believer. Two kingdoms are at work here, and the true kingdom of light is already victorious over the want-to-be kingdom of darkness. The enemy lives a fantasy of being god and a king having his kingdom. He desperately desires to be God; therefore, he will practice on the weak, wicked, insecure, and those who are thirsty for prestige and power. They have no love for you! Everything he blesses you with is linked to destruction.

Do you understand that Lucifer never wanted to be a father? He's too selfish. He destroys children; he's the devil, the adversary, the destroyer of relationships, families, and children. He wanted to be God, not a Father! When Lucifer was in heaven, he saw God as king, rich, and glorious beyond measure, The God of everything. God had everything but a son; children from his own body understand that everything God created came into existence by his spoken word, but when he looked around, He had no Son!

Jesus said, "Behold, I stand at the door (heart), and knock: if anyone hears my voice and opens the door, I will come into him, and eat with that person, and they with me" (Revelation 3:20).

This is about a relationship, a consensual spiritual relationship. God will not force Himself on any of us, no matter how much He loves us; we must accept His love and reciprocate it. We are to grow in our relationship with God; this is the reason for a consistent prayer life, reading God's word, and assembling with other believers for encouragement and strength to know you are not in this fight alone.

Being Born Again gives your soul and spirit a new start; your flesh is the house they dwell in; your flesh is not born again; your spirit is. You are putting your flesh under subjection and authority to your new spirit and Holy Spirit. You are one with God and value your relationship like a marriage.

You are betrothed or engaged now; carry yourself

in such a manner that you are spoken for. Do not allow the enemy to violate you and your covenant with God. The Holy Spirit is like your engagement ring; stay pure and faithful until your wedding day. The wedding happens when you leave this world and go to the world prepared for you from the foundations of the world.

Nothing in the past matters; you cannot change the past. Start your new life in Christ knowing you are married to Christ and your soul belongs to him; you are spoken for. You must remain loyal, dedicated, and faithful to God through Jesus Christ. To those who may not understand your new walk with God, the devil will continue on your trail because he wants you back.

You were his slave and property by thief; he stole you from God in the garden, thief by deception. God cursed the ground for our sake, meaning the stuff our bodies are made of, not our soul and spirit. Believers have so much to look forward to; you are the bride of Christ, not a harlot for the devil. DO NOT let the devil violate you! Stay with God.

Some people have played both sides and strayed

from God. You cannot serve two masters; the devil understands this, even when we don't. They may have had a dedicated life to God, praying, reading the word, and being faithful to a church or ministry. Then you look at them, and they are doing things they have never done before. Some of the things are shocking to them as they are doing them. Some things are so terrible they will never disclose them to anyone; there are no secrets between them and the devil. We know God knows everything; this is why repentance is necessary; you can return to God no matter what you have done.

Again, you must be Born Again; don't play with the devil this time! God knows and sees you if you are reading this and know this is you and feel convicted. Just humble yourself to God and repent. There is no shame in what you've done. "We all have sinned and come short of God's glory." The shame is not telling it, repenting, and starting over with a clean slate. This is the power of being Born Again.

God may require you to expose that devil who had you in bondage as a declaration of your alliance with Christ and the kingdom of God. When you are born again, knowing who feeds you and what you eat is essential. This is spiritual, not natural. You have to eat right and grow in the truth of God's word to mature to the place where you become converted. Just because you are saved doesn't mean you are converted. Judas was saved being with Jesus but did not finish the course to be converted.

When you are converted, the devil has no authority over you; you are mature enough to exercise power and authority over him. You become like Christ; leaving God is the last thing the enemy or anybody can cause you to do, and you are sold out to Jesus. Judas cut a deal with Satan for thirty pieces of silver. If we do not overcome the lust of the eye, the lust of the flesh, and the pride of life, the devil knows he has a chance to turn us against God. Peter denied Jesus because he was not yet converted. Nothing surprises God; He knows what we are going through, but we are not alone. Look at what Jesus told Simon Peter before it happened,

And the Lord said, Simon, Simon, behold, Satan hath desired to have you, that he may sift you as wheat: But I have prayed for thee, that thy faith fail not: and when thou art converted, strengthen thy brethren. And he said unto him, Lord, I am ready to go

with thee, both into prison and to death. And he said, I tell thee, Peter, the cock shall not crow this day; before that, thou shalt three times deny that thou knowest me. __ Luke__ 22:31-34

Chapter Six

Born Into It

Every human being in this world, regardless of race, creed, religion, sex, belief, or occupation, has come into existence from a man's seed and through a woman. It is undeniable that every person born in this world owes their existence in the flesh to a man and woman.

Becoming a citizen of a new country involves complying with its laws, rules, and regulations. As an American citizen, you cannot dictate your country's laws to another country to gain citizenship. If you desire to become a citizen of the Kingdom of God, it would be wise to comply with the King's laws and be thankful for the privilege of being granted citizenship.

Now, there was a man of the Pharisees named Nicodemus, a member of the Jewish ruling council. He came to Jesus at night and said, "Rabbi, we know you are a teacher who has come from God. No one could perform the miraculous signs you are doing if God were not with him." In reply, Jesus declared, "I tell you the truth, no one can see the kingdom of God unless he is born again."

"How can a man be born when he is old?" Nicodemus asked. "Surely he cannot enter a second time into his mother's womb to be born!" Jesus answered, "I tell you the truth, no one can enter the kingdom of God unless he is born of water and the Spirit. Flesh gives birth to flesh, but the Spirit gives birth to spirit. You should not be surprised at my saying, 'You must be born again.' The wind blows wherever it pleases. You hear its sound, but you cannot tell where it comes from or where it is going. So it is with everyone born of the Spirit."

"How can this be?" Nicodemus asked. "You are Israel's teacher," said Jesus, "Do you not understand these things? I tell you the truth; we speak of what we know and testify to what we have seen, but still, you people do not accept our testimony. I have spoken to you of earthly things, and you do not believe; how will you believe if I speak of heavenly things? No one

has ever entered heaven except the one who came from heaven–the Son of Man. **John 3:1-13**

Have you ever considered the power of being born again? Amazingly, we get to choose who our father will be.

"But as many as received him, to them gave he the power to become the sons of God, even to them that believe on his name: Which were born, not of blood, nor of the will of the flesh, nor the will of man, but of God." John 1:12-13

After Simon, now known as Peter, went to the upper room on the day of Pentecost and received the Holy Ghost with power, he was converted. Before this experience, Simon knew the Holy Ghost only as a comforter, not power. This experience taught him that we need both aspects of the Holy Spirit. He was never the same after receiving the Holy Ghost with power and boldness. He was addressed as Apostle Peter from then on. Many Christians get saved but do not complete the process of being converted and end up leaving, thinking it's too hard or not working. Many compromises, so they have one foot in and the other foot out, and for this reason, they do not have the power and authority over the enemy that Jesus gave us to have.

**"But ye shall receive power, after that the Holy Ghost has come upon you: and ye shall be witnesses unto me both in Jerusalem, and in all Judaea, and Samaria, and unto the uttermost part of the earth."
Acts 1:8**

The Holy Ghost or Holy Spirit is meant to give us power, but unfortunately, many preachers and pastors have studied about it without ever experiencing it themselves. This is a problem for the parishioners because these pastors may discourage them from seeking this experience with God. Remember, Jesus died so that we could have His Spirit on earth. However, some pastors and teachers have been influenced by a deceptive spirit and try to convince people that having the Holy Ghost is no longer relevant. Do not be misled by them!

"Please note the following truth: The Holy Ghost and power are available to every believer until Jesus returns and takes all of his people out of this earth, leaving it to Satan for a thousand years. Do not allow anyone to reduce the power of God to speak in tongues, as this is a trick. Speaking in tongues is only one manifestation of the Holy Ghost, and exercising your power and authority over the enemy is what Jesus ordained you to do.

The enemy will use any method to deter as many people as possible from believing they can have authority over evil. False doctrines are preached and taught to weaken the Christian's faith in the supernatural power of God's spirit. Distractions and deception enable the devil to reign free. He has taken over our families, communities, and churches - because we are not operating in power and authority. We have become great worship producers, but not the power of worship. Therefore, if you are going to be a believer or Christian, you owe it to God and yourself to go all the way and do what Jesus commands, having His Holy Spirit. After all, He died for us to have these privileges.

Why is it difficult to understand when Jesus says we must be born again of the water (symbolic of the woman) and Spirit (God's seed)? In the Kingdom of God, every person who reaches there will only do so because they were "Born Again." This is the prerequisite to living in God's world, Heaven, which is eternal. For those who reject this, Heaven is not their home; in other words, they do not belong there—those who embrace God's word and are born again become part of the family of God.

Setting aside quality time to allow God to nurture and guide you is essential for strengthening your relationship with Him. You can grow in your faith by reading God's word, fasting, and praying constantly. As you consistently engage in these spiritual practices, you'll begin to mature in your faith and ultimately become a warrior for Christ. You will not be easily persuaded to indulge in immoral and ungodly things. If you love like Jesus, Live like Jesus, and Lead like Jesus. This will enable you to help save others and guide them towards becoming more like Christ…to change the world.

We were created initially to worship God; the enemy desires more than anything to pervert our worship by us worshiping him and material things; he's hiding behind many things we pursue in life to throw us off track.

Being born again gives us a new slate; we are newborns who worship God as our Father. Anyone born of the Spirit will owe their life and existence to Jesus. Jesus said, **"You cannot see the kingdom unless you are born again; you cannot enter the kingdom unless you are born again." I AM the Way, the Truth, and the Life; no one will come to the Father unless they come through me."**

Just as every human being who has ever come to this earth has come through a woman, so will everyone from this earth who will make it to heaven come through Jesus!

Who will you believe, the One who loved us so much that He came down from heaven to redeem us by unselfishly laying down His life for us, or the rebellious One who was eternally kicked out of heaven because of his selfishness, jealousy, hatred, and pride?

Jesus, the only One who came down from heaven to save us, says," You must be Born Again." ...Now What? Will you do it? Will you be born again? It's every person's choice as to who their eternal Father will be.

If you accept Jesus as your Lord and Savior, You

are Born Again into a new life, and that life is eternal..."

Chapter Seven

Life as a Believer

The concept of being born again is powerful. It offers us a second chance at life on earth and the opportunity for eternal life with Jesus. As followers of Jesus Christ, we must prioritize our commitment to Him above all else and not merely attend church as a formality.

While it's essential to come together as one body, let us also envision the immense power we could unleash if all believers of Jesus united as a single social group, with Christ as the head. Our collective strength would be unmatched, rendering the "cancel culture" irrelevant.

Considering that only twelve men who believed in Jesus wholeheartedly and followed His instructions could turn the world upside down, it's clear that we possess immense power and authority. However, our potential is greatly diminished by our divisions. We are so divided on many levels that we are probably only using a fraction of the power and authority Heaven has given us.

Pursuing unity rather than division is crucial for a new believer, especially within any Christian group. One should refrain from being a cause for division and instead strive to be the glue that holds the group together for the sake of God.

This approach will foster a conducive environment for growth in the faith, promote harmonious relationships among believers, and enable the group to achieve its collective objectives. Therefore, embracing a unifying mindset that cultivates positive interactions, respects diversity, and upholds the values and teachings of the Christian faith is imperative. God knew you even before you were born. Before your creation, your spirit existed within God's Spirit, independent of physical characteristics such as form, sex, gender, race, or origin. It is said that God spoke something into your spirit; thus, you were created as a spirit being.

* * *

Before we were given physical bodies, God communicated messages to us in our disembodied state. As we journey through life's twists and turns, we may encounter moments that oppose the core of existence. Destiny and purpose are already within us.

You have a new life in Christ; don't fear what God will say to you through Holy Spirit. Get to know God's voice and follow Him with confidence.

Discouragement

Are you feeling lost and alone, grappling to hold on to hope? In such moments, we must find solace by reflecting on how God saved us and spared our lives from a path of degradation and sin. We possess everything when we have God and His unwavering promises, a beacon of hope in the darkest times.

Always remember this: when God makes a promise, it is not just a mere statement but a firm guarantee. No matter how impossible the situation may seem, if you hold on and believe, you will undoubtedly receive what God has promised you. Unlike humans, God never breaks His promises. Even in the face of death, He remains steadfast to His word.

* * *

God continues to fulfill His promise to Abraham: to bless his descendants and increase their numbers. Abraham was an older man without children when God first made this promise. Despite this, God promised to give him a son and grow his nation. Even after Abraham's death, God did not back out of His promise as if He had run out of time. God hovers over His word to perform it and complete what He said.

His word is an everlasting assurance of His promise to be with us, offering solace and strength during the most challenging times. He knows us better than we know ourselves.

"Are not two sparrows sold for a penny? And not one of them shall fall on the ground without your Father: but the very hairs of your head are all numbered. Fear not, therefore: ye are of more value than many sparrows." Mathew 10:29-30

(For the Father is sovereign and has complete knowledge).

We must hold on to our faith and trust in His word when we feel like giving up. John 14:8 says, "I will never leave you comfortless; I will come to you." So, hold tight to God's promises and find the strength to persevere through any challenge.

* * *

It is crucial to walk with God and never be divided over which God to serve. In this world, we are often faced with conflicting beliefs and ideologies, but we must always choose to follow the path of righteousness. It is important to note that we cannot serve God and money, as our devotion can only be to one master at a time. Therefore, ensuring that we have a healthy relationship with money and that it serves us and our purpose in life rather than vice versa is imperative.

Always Pray

- **Philippians 4:6 NIV** Do not be anxious about anything, but in every situation, by prayer and petition, with thanksgiving, present your requests to God.

- **Romans 8:26 NIV** In the same way, the Spirit helps us in our weakness. We do not know what we ought to pray for, but the Spirit himself intercedes for us through wordless groans.

- **James 5:16 NIV** Confess your sins to each other and pray for each other so that you may be healed. The earnest prayer of a righteous person has great power and produces wonderful results.

- **Matthew 18:19 NIV:** "Again, truly I tell you that if two of you on earth agree about anything they ask for, it will be done for them by my Father in heaven.

- **Matthew 21:22 NIV** If you believe, you will receive whatever you ask in prayer."

- **1 Timothy 2:8 NIV:** Therefore, men everywhere to pray, lifting up holy hands without anger or disputing.

- **Mark 11:24 NIV** Therefore, I tell you, whatever you ask for in prayer, believe that you have received it, and it will be yours. •

- **Luke 18:1 NIV** Then Jesus told his disciples a parable to show them that they should always pray and not give up.

Always talk to God. Maintaining a strong and unwavering connection with Jesus in every aspect of our lives is important. Communication with God is crucial, so we are blessed with the Holy Spirit's guidance. Sometimes, we are uncertain about what to pray for, but it is still important to pray nonetheless.

* * *

Prayer is not always about asking for things but rather about fellowship with God and showing our love for Him in the same way we would want to be loved. We should love Him because He loved us first. Our faith should not be influenced by external factors but rather by a constant factor in our daily lives. We can establish a stronger connection with God and live a meaningful and fulfilling life by staying steadfast in our beliefs.

We must strive to learn and grow stronger to inspire and guide those who will come after us. Rather than seeking to be served, we should strive to be servants. We can trust that God will reward us for our efforts. Instead of worrying about the future, we should have patience and trust in God's plan while we work towards our goals. We should remember that God knows everything we do and our challenges and will support us for His name's sake.

Be thankful for what you have and not be overwhelmed with the cares of this world to the point that they take away your peace. Peace is priceless, and it can only come when you trust in Jesus and know that God is more significant than you. God knows you better than you know yourself. Always keep this in mind for the times you may be tempted to think you can do a better job of planning your life and future.

Worship God

Understanding the importance of worshiping The One True God is crucial. We were created to worship and reflect God's image. The enemy desires nothing more than to distort that image and lead us to worship false gods that have no power over themselves.

Our God is self-existent and does not depend on any other source for His infinity. He does not need us to pick Him up and carry Him as He goes and comes as He sees fit. False gods are those things made by something or someone else and given power instead of possessing it.

If we do not worship God, we will end up worshipping something else because it is our natural tendency. As believers, it is important to be careful about who we worship. Whatever we worship with our God-given life should have the power to sustain that life eternally.

* * *

You should not outlive the god you worship. It's heartbreaking to hear news of their passing, eulogize their death, or attend their funeral. Many idolize and worship celebrities, dignitaries, or public figures who will never know them.

This is a waste of your worship, as they have no reward for you. Ultimately, they must face God and give an account for trying to be a god rather than worshiping the One True God. Worship the Creator… not the creation—Worship the God who created the universe—not the universe.

False gods are temporary, but God is forever…

Death is the great equalizer, while life in Jesus Christ is the epitome of exaltation. While we should show respect and give honor where it is due, our worship should be reserved for God and God alone. He is the first and the last, the beginning and the end. He is Alpha and Omega.

Love

- *Your greatest gift is love. "God so loved the world that He gave His only son that whoever* *believes in him will have everlasting life." **John 3:16***

- **Jesus said,** "A new command I give you: Love one another. As I have loved you, so you must love one another. **John 13:34 NIV**

- Dear friends, let us love one another, for love comes from God. Everyone who loves has been born of God and knows God.

- Whoever does not love does not know God because God is love.

- This is how God showed his love among us: He sent his one and only Son into the world that we might live through him.

- This is love: not that we loved God, but that he loved us and sent his Son as an atoning sacrifice for our sins.

- Dear friends, since God so loved us, we should also love one another. No one has ever seen God, but if we love one another, God lives in us, and his love is made complete in us.

- This is how we know that we live in him and he in us: He has given us of his Spirit.   1

John 4:7-13

As a believer in Jesus, you have been granted a new life that lasts forever. You are now a part of the kingdom of God, and your life will never be the same again. Your life no longer belongs to you because Jesus bought it with his precious blood. He is the only one who could have died for us and already finished the work. No matter what we go through in life, Jesus has already paid for it all. We belong to him now.

Remember that this world is not our home; we only pass through while representing the kingdom. You are now a part of this everlasting kingdom as a kingdom's kid. Our message and life are all about the kingdom, and we are proud to be a part of it.

"Seek you first the kingdom of God and His righteousness, and all these things will be added to you."

As a new believer, pray like this: *Our Father who is in heaven hollowed it be Your name. Your kingdom come. Your will be done on earth, as it is in heaven.*

Give us this day our daily bread, and forgive us our

trespasses, as we forgive our trespass against us. And lead us not into temptation, but deliver us from evil. For yours is the kingdom, and the power, and the glory, forever. Amen.

Scriptures For New Believers

- John 3:16 – "For God loved the world so much that he gave his one and only Son so that everyone who believes in him will not perish but have eternal life."

- 1 John 4:9-10 – "God showed how much he loved us by sending his one and only Son into the world so that we might have eternal life through him. This is real love—not that we loved God, but that he loved us and sent his Son as a sacrifice to take away our sins."

- 2 Corinthians 5:17 – "This means that anyone who belongs to Christ has become a new person. The old life is gone; a new life has begun!"

- Jeremiah 29:11 – "For I know the plans I have for you,' says the Lord. 'They are plans for good and not for disaster, to give you a future and a hope.'"

- Philippians 4:13 – "For I can do everything through Christ, who gives me strength.

- Colossians 3:17 – "And whatever you do or say, do it as a representative of the Lord Jesus, giving thanks through him to God the Father."

- Romans 10:9 – "If you openly declare that Jesus is Lord and believe in your heart that God raised him from the dead, you will be saved."

- Psalm 119:105 – "Your word is a lamp to guide my feet and a light for my path."

- Ephesians 2:8-9 – "God saved you by his grace when you believed. And you can't take credit for this; it is a gift from God. Salvation is not a reward for the good things we have done, so none of us can boast about it."

- Psalm 32:8 – "The Lord says, 'I will guide you along the best pathway for your life. I will advise you and watch over you.'"

- Matthew 28:20 – "Teach these new disciples to obey all the commands I have given you. And be sure of this: I am with you always, even to the end of the age."

- Psalm 46:1 – "God is our refuge and strength, always ready to help in times of Romans 12:2 – "Don' t copy the behavior and customs of this world, but let God transform you into a new person by changing the way you think. Then you will learn to know God' s will for you, which is good and pleasing and perfect."

- Psalm 37:4 – "Take delight in the Lord, and he will give you your heart' s desires."

- Philippians 4:6-7 – "Don' t worry about anything; instead, pray about everything. Tell God what you need, and thank him for all he has done. Then you will experience God' s peace, which exceeds anything we can understand. His peace will guard your hearts and minds as you live in Christ Jesus."

- Psalm 23:1 – "The Lord is my shepherd; I

have all that I need."

- 1 Thessalonians 5:16-18 – "Always be joyful. Never stop praying. Be thankful in all circumstances, for this is God's will for you who belong to Christ Jesus."

- Psalm 139:14 – "Thank you for making me so wonderfully complex! Your workmanship is marvelous—how well I know it."

- 1 Peter 5:7 – "Give all your worries and cares to God, for he cares about you."

- Proverbs 3:5-6 – "Trust in the Lord with all your heart; do not depend on your own understanding. Seek his will in all you do, and he will show you which path to take."

- Isaiah 41:10 — "Don't be afraid, for I am with you. Don't be discouraged, for I am your God. I will strengthen you and help you. I will hold you up with my victorious right hand."

- Isaiah 40:31 – "But those who trust in the Lord will find new strength. They will soar high on wings like eagles. They will run and not grow weary. They will walk and not faint."

- Philippians 1:6 – And I am sure that God, who began the good work within you, will continue his work until it is finally finished on the day when Christ Jesus returns."

- Joshua 1:9 — I have commanded you? Be strong and courageous! Do not be terrified or intimidated, for the Lord your God is with you wherever you go."

As a new believer, it's important to remember that reading the Bible can be overwhelming. However, there's a simple solution: find a version of the Bible that you can easily understand without deviating from the passage' s true meaning. With today's technology, you have access to Bible apps on your phone, which can be incredibly helpful. When it comes to translations, the King James Version (KJV) is the most popular because it stays true to the actual translation of the word of God. So, don't hesitate to dive into the Bible and find the version that works best for you – it's an essential part of your spiritual journey!

Below are some versions of: The HOLY BIBLE:

King James Version (KJV)
New King James Version (NKJV)
New International Version (NIV)

American Standard Version
(ASV)
English Standard Version.
(ESV)
Amplified Bible (AMP)

Below are some examples of the <u>Matthew 6:33</u> passage in different versions:

- (KJV) "But seek ye first the kingdom of God, and his righteousness; and all these things shall be added unto you."

- (NKJV) "But seek first the kingdom of God and His righteousness, and all these things shall be added to you."

- (NIV) "But seek first his kingdom and his righteousness, and all these things will be given to you as well."

- (AMP) "But first and most importantly seek (aim at, strive after) His kingdom and His righteousness (His way of doing and being right---the attitude and character of God), and all these things will be given to you also."

Prayer

Dear Heavenly Father,

As a new believer, I humbly come before you, seeking your guidance and grace on this faith journey. I am grateful for your Word that brings hope, strength, and assurance of your love for me. I pray that as I delve into the Scriptures, they become a lamp to my feet and a light to my path.

Please help me grow in my relationship with you and trust in your plans for my life. May I find comfort in your presence, and may my life testify to your love for those around me.

I fervently pray in the name of our Lord and Savior, Jesus Christ. Amen.

Note: If you have recently embarked on this new chapter of faith, we rejoice with you and congratulate you on this significant step. We eagerly await to hear from you about your decision, to pray with you, and to provide you with the necessary materials and guidance as you begin your journey with Christ.

Contact us: Kingdomrights2.org
Info@kingdomrights2.org.

"My Father's House Shall Be Called A House Of Prayer."

7 MINUTES WITH GOD PRAYER

CHALLENGE

A place where we are laying down our

phones and devices...yes, you heard me

correctly, our smart phones and

devices for just Seven (7) DEDICATED

minutes with God.

Calling on all Prayer Warriors!
We have traded praying for great production.
We are in troubling times. The world and the
church are falling apart; we must admit that we
owe God an apology and must repent.
Wherever you are in this world, as believers
let's agree to pray everyday

@ 7:00 a.m.
Whatever your time zone

INFO@KINGDOMRIGHTS2.ORG

LET'S PRAY!

www.ingramcontent.com/pod-product-compliance
Lightning Source LLC
Chambersburg PA
CBHW022207150726

47992CB00002B/994